"Chocolate Waters writes brilliantly, simply, readably, absorbably, what you were never brave enough to say for yourself, out loud in public, maybe not even brave enough to say to yourself in the public spaces inside your head. But this collection is definitely what you'd have said if you were as brave and talented and had the perfect way to capture the agony and the ecstasy of what went wrong with, what almost went right with all the relationships you've had on your way to here. Pass up this collection and you risk missing out on a conversation you needed to have with yourself to prove conclusively that you weren't the only one.

Chocolate Waters writes in your mirror. Be prepared to gasp out loud in recognition."

— SHELLY ROBERTS, Columnist,
Author of *Roberts' Rules of Lesbian Living* (Spinsters Ink Books)

also by chocolate waters

Ladies and Gentlemen: The Hudson Pier Poets,
(Eggplant Press, 2002), editor

Chocolate Waters Live & Uncensored - CD
(Eggplant Press, 2001)

Charting New Waters
(Eggplant Press, 1980)

Take Me Like A Photograph
(Eggplant Press, 1977 & 1980)

To the man reporter from the Denver Post
(Eggplant Press, 1975 & 1980)

the woman who wouldn't shake hands

chocolate waters

EGGPLANT PRESS ● **New York, New York**
POETS WEAR PRADA ● **Hoboken, New Jersey**

the woman who wouldn't shake hands

First North American Publication 2011

http://pwpbooks.blogspot.com/

Grateful acknowledgment is made to the following publications where some of these poems have or are scheduled to appear:

Big City Lit, Cedar Hill Review, Heart Pour - The Love Book (Poet Plant Press, 2011, Chris Bodor and Michael Henry Lee, eds.), *Shot Glass Journal* #5, *Skidrow Penthouse* #13, *Soundzine* #13, and *SPARK, Art From Writing: Writing From Art,* Round 4: May/June 2009 (Amy Souza, ed.).

ISBN 978-0935060096

Printed in the U.S.A.

Front cover illustration: Rosario D'Rivera
Back cover author photo: Deborah Swanger

to the ones who got away!
may they rest in peace.

introduction

with apologies to diane wakoski, whose encounter with a man she claimed she didn't even like very much inspired a book. he stayed over one night but when he left the next morning he shook her hand. wakoski got a full-length collection out of this experience and the book was called *the man who shook hands*. conversely, i never got to make love with the woman who wouldn't shake hands, a woman that i liked very much; indeed, i didn't even get the satisfaction of a handshake.

in wakoski's case, the handshake was a rebuff; in my case it would have been some acknowledgment, however slight, that there was something lovely and enticing, going on between us.

consequently, i dedicate this collection to all of us who have loved and been rejected (in other words, all of us) — whether out of the fear of loving or the fear of being loved. our disappointment at the lack of reciprocity may be bitter, but hopefully the pain, and the humor in our pain, will pave the way for something sweeter to come.

chocolate waters

contents

begin

you came that night
you came up to me
that night i
caught
your eye
that night you
caught me

acting like chocolate waters

without chocolate waters
acting
like she likes chocolate
which she does
actually
tho she likes women better
than she likes chocolate
but don't tell anyone
don't tell that woman that
she's the one chocolate
likes
more than chocolate
that's how chocolate
waters
acts

plunge

don't wanna be no
straight girl's experiment
do i?
done that before
haven't i?
how did that work out
for you?
didn't you
get it
handed back
to you?
did you
care?
did you
get it
then?
are you
getting it now?
are you getting hot now?
you are aren't you?
you
silly
fool

played my hand

doing so well
keeping my mouth shut
silencing the urge
to tell you
anything
afraid
my approach
bull-in-a-china shop
offensive
distasteful
thinking
you need safety
then
you sent
those pictures
of the dog
beautiful
but you near by
stunned me
so
dazzling
so
oh
my breath
stopped
my
mouth
went running off

i didn't mean to

scare you
please forgive
me

here i am at 60

my arms are sagging
just like mom's
like grand mom's
like the hanging gardens of
babylon
sadness underneath
my eyes
stayed there
turned
into these squashy pillows
unappealing my
tummy needs
a lot of tucks
there are days
i want to put my head
inside a paper bag
and what the hell is that
beneath my chin
a chicken neck
heck
i got the whole
damn chicken
yet
i can see you
kinder than i ever did
i can give you
softer than i ever have
i can see you honest i
can choose you i can
dare i say it
love
you i
can i
can

those bags

these bags
under my eyes are
either from
all the tears i
haven't cried or
vodka

lover fans

many lovers

have been fans
oohing and ahhing
their way in
an ego trip
you are coming over
i will slip a drink
into your hand
smooth your day
soothe you w/the chicken soup
i made myself
spinach salad

made that too
tiny routine gestures

small yet
big for me

to give
instead of take
are they enough
to hold you
will you take
them
can they
embrace you?

phone vodka

like phone sex
w/out the sex
like vodka
w/ice
over the phone
two women
two souls
conversation
sacred
profane
w/olives or
w/out
and in between:
worlds

dear joan

trying not to go there
predictable rejection
more to do w/you
than me
trying not to go there
old and stabbing feeling
never good enough
rich enough
handsome enough
never quite enough
trying not to go there
knowing this rejection
it's really you
that you're rejecting
not me

desire

chopped down
like the tree that
crashes
in the forest
what's the sound
desire makes as it
comes
crashing
down
as it never gets to come
as it crashes
down
do you hear the sound
desire
doesn't get to
make

NO. NEVER!

no never stopped me before
why now?
spent a ton of years
in supplication to the
feminine
yeah the masculine too
truth be told
i've got less years ahead
gonna be dead
soon perhaps
before i go i
just want
a simple
YES
damn it

last of the red hot idiots

boy did i get that wrong
thought i was the bull
in the china shop
bully for me
bully for you   not
that you're a bully
or an idiot
that'd be me
red hot
idiot me

all burned out

pretty is

as pretty does
and pretty
pretty much does
as she damn well pleases
pretty is as pretty does and
you are pretty
much
of the time but not this time
this time you are
pretty much
well
clueless

fantasy sucks
my dick

i had this fantasy i was
sucking your dick
only you don't have a dick

i had this fantasy
i was licking your prick
and i didn't even mind it
in fact i kind of liked it
i said kind of

i had this fantasy
i was kissing your dick
yes i kissed your dick
and i liked it

only you don't have a prick
and i'm not into dick
or dildos of any sort
ick

so what
does this say about
what i think about ....
what i think
about
        you/...
                me/...
                        dick? ...

karma/shmarma

those 2 other times
we weren't supposed to meet
you might as well have been
a bug at my feet
for all the attention i
flicked at you
why now
when
i deserve someone willing
to meet
me
evenly
raise me higher
as i'd like to do
for you silly violet
we've spent our lives vying
for position
trying
to get bigger
it's been trying
not to get smaller
you listened
to that horseshit
posed for it
married it
suffered thru it
birthed it
loved it/loathed it
stop it
silly violet
stop shrinking

entanglement

who wants to feel
this
not me
don't want to feel
one fucking thing
for you
just like mom
who wouldn't
know a feeling
if she fell over one
what chance did she have
that era   that time
that knew so much nothing
she stuffed every feeling
down the throat of that
turkey of a childhood
that awful childhood
that sent her screaming
that appalling man
who was her father
my grandfather
dreadful drunken shit head of a man
didn't know any better ?
his own demons biting him
so he bit everyone back
everyone
close to him
back you angry insufferable
dog of a man you
bit the feeling right out of
my mom
who then had none for
me

my dad
my siblings
my my my
she ran
silent as a lamb
away from one miserable man
into the arms of another
miserable man
my father
man!
and now you think
i feel something for you
just some crazy woman who
feels something for you
maybe not
maybe that would be my
mother
trying to feel
something
for
herself

dangerous

first glance
she's incredible
strong and funny
quite intelligible
second glance
she *gets* funny
scrape the surface
not delicious
she turns vicious
first glance
she's incredible

here i am writing

another poem that makes
me want to
vomit
up the desire i have for women who
are so sick they
have nothing
to give

what the hell is the matter
with me   how long
do i have to keep reliving my parents'
dysfunction
how she "loved" him so much
she couldn't … (fill in the blank) …

how he "loved" her so much
he couldn't
help
but be disappointed

how their words bashed
each other silly

silly me
listening on the steps
outside their bedroom
thinking i could ever
love

anyone

brutal

your words
painted *me* a
narcissist
hateful   stupid
stupidly hatefully
unconscious
egotist
when
all i
wanted
was...

your back

standing in front of
that soup
it was awful
the soup
not your back
i stood in back
of your back
my left hand
touched
your hip
slipped
off
into the distance
the curve of your
neck
i moved away
sat on the edge
of my bed
alone

alone

coward

narcissist

i think about myself
about myself
about my beautiful self
and my dog
my beautiful dog
my beautiful selfless dog
and my son
and my son my
beautiful
what's-his-name son
who's not as beautiful
as my dog
my beautiful dog
my beautiful sunny dog
and my ex who's
now much less
beautiful
than my dog
or my son
oh my
beautiful dog
my beautiful dog god
i love my
dog

stick out neck

chop it off
that's the risk
lop it off
loud and clear
yes i hear
got it my dear
stick out neck
chop it off

sorry

i am sorry
my sorry ass
is really effin' sorry
that it is so
pitifully sorry
that i am
so pathetically sorry
damn
i am
sorry that i
am
so damn
sorry

scrabble on

leaning tower of babylon
how you do go on and on
how you don't wanna get it on

yes i know it's babel
tower of rabble
was it leaning on and on
my how you do
babble on
and on

you wanna play scrabble
let's scrabble
scrabble on

surrender

don't think about me
seeping in
to your skin
sleeping in
under your skin
little lamb
supple skin
think about inches
more & more inches
big fat thickset inches
sticking in
shoving in
don't think
about me
don't let me
slip
under your skin
don't let   yourself
in

wow

that's how you felt?
that's how you felt me?
heard me   didn't
that's how you didn't
hear me   how i
heard you   didn't
wow
ow

SAW

she saw me like a massacre
the texas chain saw massacre
slaughtering
her like SAW
like all the SAWs 1 2 3 4 5
AND 6
that's how she
saw me

personal

whatever happened
between us was
SO
personal

that's why i
have to tell it
SO
loudly

coda

thanks
for turning me on i
was so
off
so inside/shut
down/so
turned round
so this side down
thank you
for the chance
to feel
some
thing   any
thing
again it
won't be/my last

p.s.

what i really wanna say is
what an ass you are
for not letting me
love you
for not letting me
even try

p.p.s

what i really wanna say
is what an ass i am
for not
letting you
love
me
for not letting
you
even
try

about the author

Chocolate Waters is one of the first openly lesbian poets to publish widely during the second wave of feminism, and her contribution is documented in *Feminists Who Changed America 1963-1975* (University of Illinois Press, Barbara Love, ed.). A pioneer in women's publishing and in the art of performance poetry, she has toured throughout the U.S. but makes her home in Manhattan. Her three earlier collections: *To the man reporter from the Denver Post*, *Take Me Like A Photograph* and *Charting New Waters* were produced by Eggplant Press during 1975-80 and are considered classics of the early women's movement. Her CD, *Chocolate Waters Uncensored*, which spans three decades of groundbreaking work, was released by Eggplant Productions in 2001.

Waters is the recipient of a New York State Foundation for the Arts fellowship in Poetry and has also been awarded a grant from the Barbara Deming Memorial Fund. In 1995 she was one of five featured artists in the "Artist As Citizen" exhibit, curated by Amy Ernst, at the American Council for the Arts in NYC. She has also been awarded a "fruitie" for the best poetry performance in the 2006 Fresh Fruit Festival held in Manhattan.

Her work, which has been nominated for several Puschcart prizes, has appeared in nearly a thousand publications, most recently in *Sinister Wisdom*; *Skidrow Penthouse*; *MÖBIUS, The Poetry Magazine*; *and The Enigmatist*. She has also been anthologized in *Mom – Candid memoirs by lesbians about the first woman in their life* (Alyson Books, Nisa Donnelly & Donna Allegra, eds.), *Stand Up Poetry: the Anthology*, (California State University Press, Charles Harper Webb, ed.), *The Second Word Thursdays Anthology* (Bright Hill Press, Bertha Rogers, ed.) and in *My Lover is A Woman* (Ballantine Books, Leslea Newman, ed). Newer work can be found on the internet at *Creative Women, 2River View, The Pedestal Magazine, Stirring, Samsara Quarterly,*

Poetry Magazine. and *The Astrophysicist's Tango Partner Speaks,* among others.

Hailed as the "Poet Laureate of Hell's Kitchen," Waters teaches poetry workshops, tutors individual clients and directs Eggplant Submissions – a submission service for professional poets. She makes her home in Manhattan where she is a frequent participant in the New York poetry circuit.

Contact her at website:

> http://chocolatewaters.com

or on Facebook:

> http://www.facebook.com/chocolate.waters

about the artist

Rosario D'Rivera, born in Havana, Cuba in 1960, defected to the United States in 1968. My background in the arts is, you could say 'inherited'. Coming from an artistic family, where love for music and art were at the forefront of our existence. Painting became my ultimate passion and my passion's medium consists of many things ... pen and ink, watercolors, pencils, acrylics and anything else I can use to create. These mediums change and develop according to the imagination and its choice. The images you see are joyful, playful and fun, meant to simply place a smile on your face and make the heart skip a beat. If just one of my pieces causes that feeling ... my artistic goal has been fulfilled.

As always I tell people ... take a look, a GOOD look ... and enjoy the ride!

Rosario
May 2010

Visit her at http://www.rosariodrivera.com

about the photographer

Deborah Swanger and her partner, Sharon Shomo, own Deborah Swanger Photography located in Mount Joy, Pennsylvania. Together they photograph and create portraits and fine art photography. Says Deborah, "The inexpressible power of a photograph speaks no words, yet talks to all." Visit them on the web at http://www.deborahswanger.com.